"Required Reading for Business and Healthcare Professionals!"

POWER TEAMS

The New SQUARE ROOT MODEL™
That Changes *Everything!*

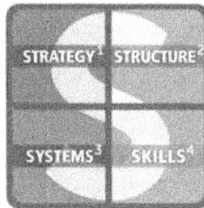

STRATEGY[1] STRUCTURE[2]

SYSTEMS[3] SKILLS[4]

Best Seller

Deb Spicer

FOUNDER, QUANTUM LEVEL SUCCESS

Published by Quantum Level Success

Copyright © 2011 by Quantum Level Success

Graphics design by Linda Brandt, BrandtRonat, Inc.

Editing Services by Sarah Spicer, SpicerProductions

Legal Consulting: Donald C. Holmes, Esq.

ISBN: 978-0-615-54910-1

DEDICATION

This book is dedicated to
M. Jane Donnini
the most spirited, dearest and
bravest woman I have ever known.

TABLE OF CONTENTS

INTRODUCTION

Prior to my decades of work in global, publicly-traded and dual listed businesses, my career began in healthcare as a Registered Nurse. After six months of work in the Neonatal Intensive Care Unit, I was chosen to join the helicopter and ambulance team to transport high-risk newborns back to our hospital. This continued for seven years until the birth of my daughter, and a couple of years later, my son.

During the following years while racing on mommy-track, I returned to college and received a Bachelor of Science Degree in Health Communications. I committed a small amount of time to health care consulting, some volunteer work, and a little public speaking, which kept my career skills current.

Back On Career Track

Once my children were enrolled full-time in elementary school, I completed the commitment I made to myself to secure an advanced degree. Obtaining the Master of Science Degree from Mercer University, Stetson School of Economics in Health Care Policy and Public Administration coincided with major changes taking place in the healthcare industry, including the transition to managed care systems and related pay for performance metrics. At that time, independent local community and rural hospitals were transitioning to regional systems with local origins. Today, many have been replaced with larger For-Profit corporations. In the For-Profit healthcare corporation, healthcare is the business. Many corporate medical operations parallel business practices that promote quality, efficiency, and operational functions to drive patient-centeredness and high-performance team delivery.

> *"Life is a great big canvas, and you should throw all the paint on it you can."*
>
> —Danny Kaye
> (American actor, singer, dancer, and comedian.)

As I finished my Master's degree, one of my part-time positions was to serve as a spokesperson on women's healthcare issues. As a healthcare spokesperson, I grew my database of press contacts and gained a great deal of regional and national media coverage. Knowing my combined background in healthcare and public relations, a colleague recommended me for a corporate position in a Fortune-500 telecommunications company. My first assignment was to leverage all regional, national and international media for the $20 million this company had invested in the 1996 Atlanta Summer Olympic Games. In the months following the Summer Olympics Closing Ceremonies, our teams were recognized with multiple media and public relations awards.

Move to Public Relations

I left telecommunications years later to join a global public relations firm. For more than a decade I worked with or for global, publicly-traded, dual-listed, multi-lingual, multi-cultural businesses, where my role was to lead global teams to achieve their objectives. I worked in industries such as data management, enterprise computer hardware, logistics and supply chain, telecommunications, energy, and aerospace.

Today's Challenge

Technology advances and the tightening global economy have led to the fact that employees can be dispersed across regions and throughout the world. Telecommuting, flexible schedules and the prevalence of satellite offices closer to key customers create the challenge of virtual teaming. Employees spread across wide territories generate a new dimension of complexity, especially when it comes to building team cohesiveness and addressing work-related, interpersonal issues.

In this emerging world of globally dispersed employees, how do you implement consistency and quality in business and healthcare cultures? What does it take to drive one global strategy? How do you build cohesive, productive, profitable teams? How do you WIN?

The easy answer: **It takes the creation and execution of high-performance teams.**

The hard answer: **It takes the creation and execution of high-performance teams.**

Effective Teams

As a Six-Sigma project leader, I learned first-hand that effective teamwork does not just happen, particularly when a team is inherited or cobbled together bringing different cultures, different operating processes, and different perspectives about customer service delivery. Six-Sigma business processes (a method that enables companies to increase profits dramatically by streamlining operations, improving quality, eliminating variables and fixing defects) engage cross-functional and globally dispersed members from diverse reporting structures. By mixing public relations (PR) leaders with human resources (HR) representatives or marketing managers with engineers, or sales representatives with finance managers (to name a few examples), drives a particular solution and adds three-dimensional, game-changing effects.

Over the years, I discovered and capitalized on the core components within **THE SQUARE ROOT MODEL™** that directly influence the creation and success of high power teams. Additionally, I utilized the **TOOLS™** within **THE SQUARE ROOT MODEL™** to meet the team challenges I personally experienced; the same challenges many of you as leaders deal with daily. What I am offering in writing this book is to share with you and other leaders **THE SQUARE ROOT MODEL™** and its associated **SQUARE ROOT TOOLS™**. As a leader, you can implement these **TOOLS™** to sustain and improve individual and team contributions to benefit your team, and the success of your organization.

> *"Whatever you vividly imagine, ardently desire, sincerely believe and enthusiastically act upon must inevitably come to pass."*
>
> —Paul J. Meyer
> (Founder, Success Motivation Institute)

STRATEGY[1] STRUCTURE[2]

SYSTEMS[3] SKILLS[4]

1

THE SQUARE ROOT MODEL^{TM}

Building Power Teams

"No one can dispute the power teamwork delivers to an organization. When people come together and set aside their individual needs for the good of the whole, they get more done in less time and with less cost; the whole is greater than the sum of the part."

– Patrick Lencioni
(Author of national best-seller
The Five Temptations of a CEO)

A s leaders, we know first-hand that achieving goals takes drive, determination and focused persistence. And we know the same is required to create, lead and build high-performance teams. So what do high-performance teams look like? What are the characteristics and behaviors of team members that are highly-effective?

High Performance Teams

If we have been fortunate, we have experienced high-performance teams that operate with excitement, purpose, passion, and creativity. We know how it feels when teams we are on are completely engaged and communicate in free-flowing conversations. We feel safe enough within the team to involve each other in tough discussions and decision-making. In high-performance teams, leaders and our team members collaborate freely, demonstrate no barriers or judgments against each other and willingly accept the thoughts and opinions offered by one another. This acceptance speeds up success, growth, innovation, partnerships and accountability; all is given freely and effortlessly. In the end leaders know and can feel that these high-performance teams are increasing value to one another, the team itself, and the organization as a whole.

Dysfunctional Teams

On the other end of the spectrum are those teams we have experienced that are ripe with politics, bureaucracies and hidden agendas. Anyone who has been in a management position for any length of time has encountered his/her fair share of difficult employee behaviors. The degree of difficulty can vary from downright infuriating to outright disruptive. Political, bureaucratic, and agenda-driven behaviors disrupt and sabotage the other team members and leaders. These team members clearly demonstrate that they will do whatever it takes to fulfill their ulterior motives. They will give no recognition or value to anyone else because by their actions they demonstrate that they are only looking out for themselves. When the other team members see this behavior, they walk on eggshells and hold back their thoughts, ideas and contributions to the team.

In team settings, you cannot let personnel issues fester. Negative behaviors need to be dealt with immediately even though addressing difficult conduct may make you feel uncomfortable. It is highly unproductive as the leader to put off dealing with negative behaviors on the team, as this kills momentum and success.

Solutions

What do you do when you can't always use authority to get people to cooperate? How can you use influence to get others to be involved and help solve the initiates at hand? What are the core components that directly influence the success of highly-effective teams?

Through years of participating on and leading teams, I have learned first-hand how to neutralize and remove negative behaviors and capitalize on positive conduct within a team. I offer this **MODEL™** and these **TOOLS™** to help you leverage your own teams for success.

In the **SQUARE ROOT MODEL™**, there are four key components: **STRATEGY**[1], **STRUCTURE**[2], **SYSTEMS**[3] and **SKILLS**[4]. Rooted within these key components (as the diagram illustrates) are the **SQUARE ROOT TOOLS™** that, when leveraged and applied to team dynamics in business and healthcare cultures, promotes high-performance achievement.

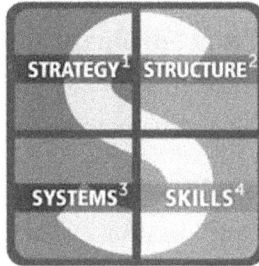

THE SQUARE ROOT MODEL™

Ultimately, the goal is to capitalize on the four components (**STRATEGY**[1], **STRUCTURE**[2], **SYSTEMS**[3] and **SKILLS**[4]) that incorporate strong talent, energy, resources, and ideas to create powerful, high-performing teams. Which of these four components is more important? Are your lungs more important than your heart or your liver? Just as you have to have all of your body parts working together to add value (and avoid illness) you need all components within **THE SQUARE ROOT MODEL™** to succeed. This is what I mean:

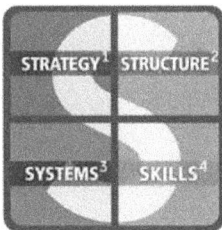

THE SQUARE ROOT MODEL™: When applied in business or healthcare team settings, is fundamentally useful in building successful high-performance teams. Each teams' purpose is to find solutions that contribute directly to the achievement of its unit, its division, or its region, to ensure that the organization succeeds.

STRATEGY[1]: The core approach the organization will use to achieve its goals. It is the distinct plans, methods or series of actions the organization will take in order to succeed in the marketplace. From a team-strategy perspective, it is how the structure, systems and skills will be integrated to ensure that what the team delivers moves the company in the right direction.

STRUCTURE[2]: The way in which the people in the organization are positioned, coordinated, or aligned to utilize their skills and strengths. In the team structure, it is the inclusion of key functions and the arrangement of the individuals so that all of the parts create valuable input, and together they deliver more to drive the future success of the company.

SYSTEMS[3]: A menu of coordinated methods that drive overall company success. Utilizing the menu of available components within **SYSTEMS** allows the leader to manage the team's energy, creativity, knowledge, experience and commitment to achieve its objectives. The available methods that can be utilized include compensation, bonus structure, performance appraisals, promotions, dotted-line and skip-level reporting, exit strategies and early-retirement packages.

SKILLS⁴: The excellence of knowledge, talent, ability, practice, competence, experience and spirit of cooperation an individual brings to the team. **SKILLS⁴** include the unique capabilities or key elements that collectively drive higher team productivity, and contribute to the enterprise's goals.

The Real World

Ideally, a leader would be able to choose the individuals and the make-up of their team. Often though, leaders inherit team members and *then* begin the process of shaping the team into one that supports the success of the company. As a successful leader you are in the unique position to help your teams build strong relationships, foster internal commitment to the mission and direction of the company, and you can place a strong emphasis on communications, both in speaking and in listening. And you can support your team's commitment to, and their success in, driving achievable, measurable, and bottom-line results.

In every leader's ideal world, your team members are able to perform at a high level right away; they are highly-motivated, highly-skilled and highly-productive. The reality? Sometimes there are great performers, sometimes there are questionable ones, and sometimes there are those who just don't belong because they cannot do the job.

Leader's Energy

It is often stated that the real job as the team leader is to assemble the right people, set direction, communicate it and then get out of the way to *let* people do their jobs. The initial energy the leader must devote to the team to achieve this dynamic far exceeds that which is returned by the team. It requires a high level of energy to cultivate full team buy-in, to drive team cohesion, and to nurture an environment where the best of each team member can be contributed. It takes time for the team's energy and that of the leader's to "equalize". However, when teams blend, they become highly motivated, take initiative and are more productive. When this happens, a prevailing energy is created and the amount of energy invested by the leader is matched or exceeded by the team's drive and the powerful content it delivers.

As a team leader, it is our responsibility to remove obstacles that impede the energy and progress of the team. It is realistic to consider that a team member may not be able to step-up in attitude, behavior, or skill and a decision may have to be made to remove a non-performer. As leaders, we know the faster our teams get up to speed the more they will drive our teams' objectives and achieve our companies' goals.

"The leader's role is to be the chief energy officer. It is to mobilize and focus and direct and inspire and regularly recharge those he or she leads."

–Tony Schwartz
(Speaker/Author:
The Way We Are Working Isn't Working)

For a FREE PDF download of the SQUARE ROOT TOOLS^{TM}

Quick Reference Guide

Click Here or Go To: www.QuantumLevelSuccess.com

2

"I'M FROM CORPORATE...
...AND I'M HERE TO HELP"

"When you think of fierce conversation, think passion, integrity, authenticity, and collaboration. Think cultural transformation. Think leadership."

–Susan Scott
(Best-selling author of *Fierce Conversations*)

A ny time there is major corporate change, it is likely to be met with some form of resistance. Regardless of what leadership role you hold, **THE SQUARE ROOT TOOLS™** will prove influential in leveraging excellence from your teams which in turn, will increase value to your organization.

When I was recruited to join the management team of a $4-billion company, our overarching challenge was to lead a successful global turnaround in three years. The turnaround included driving a single-brand and implementing global standard operating procedures that would create better value and be consistent across all regions. This major change would meet our customers' needs in the changing global marketplace.

Transformation

Many factors contributed to the need for this significant and effective transition. First, the development of the deeper global economy and associated market changes were underlying factors. At that time, our company operated as if it were 42 individual companies. Market penetration was mixed, business models varied, pricing and billing processes were individualized by country, and IT systems were neither standardized nor globalized. While we enjoyed successful and long-term relationships with the world's largest brands in this industry, our operating processes were cumbersome, confusing and inconsistent. To support our customers' needs and keep pace with their expectations required us to make changes to both our strategies and operating structures.

Overall, the management team shared ownership for these turnaround initiatives. Six-Sigma was introduced and cross-functional, cross-regional global teams were formed and led by management leaders.

Getting Started

During the introductory face-to-face meeting with the global team I acquired, we conducted the necessary introductions and icebreaker exercises. While I was new to the company, I found that many of the team members were long-time employees that had never met each other. Since this company historically operated as single, individual entities, there had been no reason for these employees to collaborate or operate together. They had all been hidden behind the very borders that needed to be removed immediately.

Now, when frontline staff hears the words, "I'm from corporate and I'm here to help", it is quite probable that the majority automatically think, "Oh, great! What can you possibly know?" or similar rejecting attitude. As the leader, you may have the best of intentions. However, no amount of charisma, intelligence or magnetism can erase this phenomenon. Knowing that these natural, resistant reactions exist, helps leaders know how to plan for the right sequential team-building processes.

During the same face-to-face meeting, the most important agenda item was to deeply engage the team in open and direct discussion about how we could operate and succeed as a global "virtual team". The act of openly discussing how we would work together regularly in order to achieve our initiatives was another catalyst that signaled to them the interruption of *"business-as-usual."*

My **STRATEGY**[1] was to build a platform that encouraged and allowed for open, honest dialogue. This made it possible for us to discuss how we would interact, how we would openly receive each other's ideas, how we would be skeptical, question and not accept statements at face-value, how we would make decisions, and how we would collectively manage ourselves successfully, while simultaneously remaining in our respective "homes" around the globe.

It was important to keep the current reporting structure in place, where each team member continued to report to his or her respective leader. What changed was the implementation of a cross-departmental, cross-cultural team **STRUCTURE**[2]. This was a necessary process that allowed the company to operate on a global scale.

New **SYSTEMS**[3] needed to be put in place. First, we focused on what conditions make meetings successful. Understanding, "What can we do *together* so no one's time is wasted?" and "How can we agree to be responsible to each other?", sets the foundation for developing the important ground rules of how our teams will be reliable and trustworthy to each other.

Ground Rules

The list below recognizes some of the ground rules that were utilized in our team meetings. Together we decided on these rules to help address the business initiatives we were required to develop, and set the standard for the cooperative tone and conduct we would use when we met.

- Meetings will start and end on schedule, on time.

- Ask questions and focus on the issues without making personal attacks or without a challenging attitude
- Bring out the best ideas in others
- Share information without "knowing-all-the-answers"
- Build on each other's opinions
- Address disagreement without arguing
- Listen openly to others' opinions
- Make suggestions without bossing others
- Summarize progress
- Collectively enforce these terms for the success of the team

Under this structure, each person begins to contribute to discussions. They become self-sanctioned and adhere to the terms, becoming empowered to take responsibility to help enforce the parameters under which the team operates. When doing this, a striking change happens; the *team* becomes the enforcer, which builds solidarity and group loyalty (promoting a *healthy* way to deal with opposition) which empowers the team to "push-back" when needed.

Leader Reliability

In addition to setting our ground rules, I described in the first meeting what the team could expect from me. For one, the team could rely on nearly 24/7 availability. While I traveled often and members did not always know in which country (or time zone) I was in, they were encouraged to communicate, communicate, communicate. I adhered to my vow by promptly returning calls and emails.

When team members agree to be reliable to each other and are predictable in how they will act during the time they work together, trust is built, and trust is fundamental in building a powerful, successful team. As leaders, we know that creating and nurturing effective team dynamics also requires building trust between the team and the leader. The need to build trust is true whether we are sitting in the office next to

each other or in an office on another continent. This becomes expo-
nentially more important when leading team members who are spread
out around the world.

Formidable Challenge

Creating a unified, global team culture is a formidable challenge. On our
team, we found that we could successfully conduct weekly global conference calls and reach almost everyone during their regular office
hours, with the exception of the United States where I was based. This
required my commitment to lead the call at 4:00 AM Eastern Standard
Time (EST), which connected with those in England, across Europe and
in South Africa during their morning office hours and at the end of the
work day in Australia. (The team members located in the morning
zones would ask the Australian members if we were going to have a
good day, since those in Australia were almost done with their work-
day.) As an early riser, 4:00 AM EST was not a conflict for me, yet it demonstrated tremendous leadership commitment. It met the team on their
terms, instead of requiring team members to adapt to "corporate con-
venience" or a "top-down" management style often found in corporations. Also, we created the format so that over time each team member
was able to "host" a meeting. This required me to travel to the members'
respective offices whether it was in Australia, Europe or South America. By being on-site, the team member and I were able to "bond" and I
was able to assess commitment and follow-through, and evaluate what
obstacles needed to be removed to improve our team's success.

Top-down management styles are as prevalent in healthcare settings as they are in corporate cultures. Nurses, technicians, and healthcare providers who are assigned to evening and night-shifts are often frustrated when mandatory trainings and department meetings are conducted during day-shift hours. The requirement is that these staff members are always required to come in during their off-hours (which, for some, means during their regular sleep cycle) to participate in trainings or meetings, which feels heavy-handed and unfair. When possible, the charge nurse or unit leader can meet his or her night-shift staff on their terms by adjusting the mandatory meeting schedule to begin early in the morning (by occasionally asking the day-shift to come in an hour early), or by requesting the night-shift to come in one hour earlier (instead of in the middle of the day), to participate in the meeting together with the evening-shift staff.

Commitment / Accountability / Trust

My on-site presence demonstrated commitment, accountability and built trust. Furthermore, it created an opportunity to boost emotions, increase motivation, improve perceptions and make progress in meaningful ways. The more each team member experienced progress and small wins, the more likely he or she was to contribute productively.

When building the cross-continental teams, it was important to reinforce the **SKILLS⁴** that each individual team member possessed. In any team setting, by focusing on individual strengths and skillsets, team members feel empowered (which builds confidence), each member sees value in the other (which builds respect), and therefore, each team member feels safe to contribute individually (as there now exists trust in one another.) Now you have team cohesion.

Due to the SARS epidemic in 2003, travel restrictions were imposed for several weeks and therefore travel to my teams' offices was halted. However, by that time our team had coalesced. We were able to continue our momentum through weekly conference calls, and the team was working well enough together that my physical presence was no longer necessary. Leadership travel to the front-lines is instrumental in promoting a "we are in this together" tone, and removes any hint of corporate repression.

Corporate Culture Change

Changing a corporate culture is a complicated process and cannot be planned or implemented by a small number of top executives. Our responsibility was to build (for the first time in this company's history) effective and efficient global teams. We faced a new direction. Being able to work together with others from around the globe, and from different functions within the organization, was fundamental to achieving the changes necessary in order to succeed. No one within the company was exempt from contributing to its success, which in and of itself was game-changing.

The open, accepting culture built into our team allowed for diversity, which provided unique insights, alternative views, and revealed assumptions that could be clarified or refuted immediately. Most importantly, the process of open communication and boundary setting promotes and encourages sharing and the free-exchanges of feelings, thoughts, ideas and creative solutions. This is your foundation for a team's long-term success, and a principle of leading, made powerful when practiced: Lead By Example.

"Example is not the main thing in influencing others. It is the only thing."

–Albert Einstein

(German-born theoretical physicist and Nobel Peace Prize winner who developed the theory of general relativity, which effected a revolution in physics. Yes, that one.)

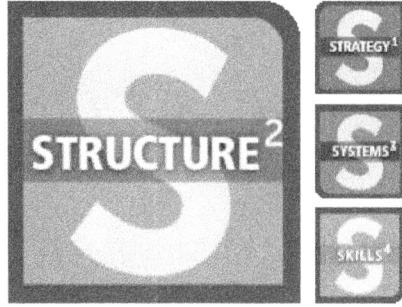

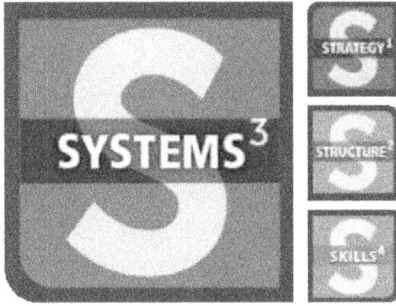

3

THE SQUARE ROOT TOOLS™

LEVERAGING YOUR TEAM FOR EXCELLENCE

"Build for your team a feeling of oneness, of dependence on one another and of strength to be derived of unity."

–Vince Lombardi

(Best known for his successes as NFL football coach with two Super Bowl wins and five NFL Championships.)

I n this and the following chapters you will learn how **THE SQUARE ROOT MODEL™** empowers team leaders in building highly-effective teams. This **MODEL™**, and the associated **SQUARE ROOT TOOLS™**, aids leaders in gaining positive momentum and systematically accelerates team understanding and action on a new vision, a new direction or a new culture. Whether in business or in healthcare, these **TOOLS™** promote accountability up and down the organization and focus team members and the organization on passionate delivery for its customers' and/or patients' success.

THE SQUARE ROOT MODEL™

In Chapter One, **THE SQUARE ROOT MODEL™** described the four core components that influence high-performance teams, (**STRATEGY[1], STRUCTURE[2], SYSTEMS[3] and SKILLS[4].**)

By combining two of the four **SQUARE ROOT MODEL™** components, you have access to 12 **TOOL™** combinations. As the leader, you can use these **TOOLS™** to amplify specific behaviors that will promote excellence on your team, or you can use other **TOOLS**™ to address dysfunctional team conduct.

THE SQUARE ROOT TOOLS™

Strengthening Your Leadership Confidence

In each **SQUARE ROOT TOOL**™ one component serves as the primary approach, and the other as the secondary. As the leader, you can choose which **TOOL**™ will best meet the team challenges you are facing head-on in order to magnify and reinforce positive team behaviors and outcomes. These **TOOLS**™ are designed to help you build the strongest most successful teams, while both building and preserving confidence within your personnel. And for *you*, these **TOOLS**™ are designed to strengthen your confidence and success in confronting negative behaviors.

On the following pages I will provide at least one example in order to help you understand the options you have as the leader. So buckle up your tool belt, as we walk through each one to discover how to actively engage *your* teams and deliver the greatest impact in accelerating each business's success.

4

COMPETING FACTIONS WITHIN A TEAM

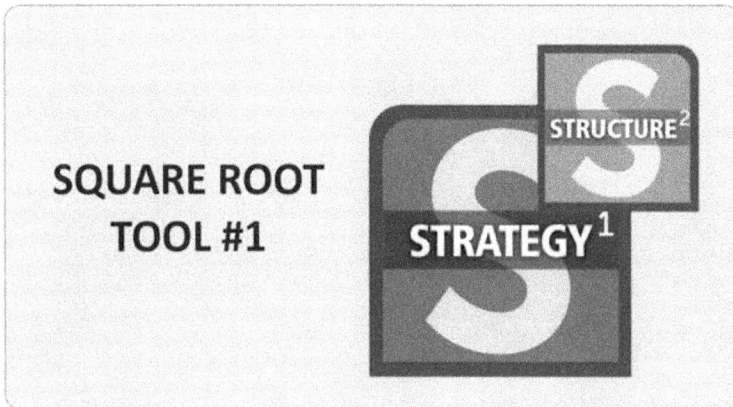

SQUARE ROOT TOOL #1

STRUCTURE^2

STRATEGY^1

"Communication goes beyond the words we choose."

–Tony Jeary

(Public speaker and coach to CEOs)

⌘

EXAMPLE: A global, cross-company, cross-functional team was appointed to ensure that key business processes and drivers were incorporated into the new SAP technology platform being built to address their customers' and the company's global needs. While there was representation on the team from sales, operations, marketing, finance, billing, accounting and collections, it was the IT business developers and the IT quality assurance members that presented strong and competing positions about the right path on which to move forward in addressing this initiative.

KEY ISSUES:

1. Two opposing groups both extremely passionate about their viewpoints.

2. The need to blend the two groups into the existing team.

GOALS:

- To address the challenge of competing factions within this team.
- To rebuild the team to be cohesive and high-performing.

STRATEGY[1]: *The core approach the organization will use to achieve its goals.*

While it may sound surprising, the **STRATEGY[1]** here was to *encourage* the free-exchange of information and provide the platform for the two opposing groups to compete, but only initially. Encouraging the two groups to present their side's viewpoints emboldens the opposing players; each side plays-off each other, drawing out the strongest, most creative ideas, and the most diverse perspectives. (When engaging the two sides in their competitive sparring, the leader's role is to maintain the focus of these discussions within the framework of the organization's priorities and direction, while still maintaining a professional and respectful atmosphere.)

Merge Opposing Groups

Once the competing ideas and proposed solutions are exhausted, the leader can change the dynamic and work to merge the two opposing groups with the rest of the members in order to form a single, mutually reinforcing team.

STRUCTURE[2]: *How people in the organization are positioned, coordinated and aligned to utilize their skills and strengths.*

In our example, once all ideas and perspectives from the competing members were exhausted, I was able to use **STRUCTURE[2]** to change the competitive environment. In this case, we created sub-groups for the purpose of disbanding the factions and blending the team together. With this new structure, we began building a team dynamic of inclusion while promoting the free-exchange of the team members' thoughts and contributions.

In a mixed, cross-functional *STRUCTURE²*, the leader can involve the team collectively in probing and analyzing each idea to see if the rationale and answers offered earlier by the opposing teams makes sense. As a team, members can verify, validate, or add more information to inject new perspectives and content and refine the ideas to develop the best solutions for the company.

BENEFIT: The *STRATEGY¹/STRUCTURE²* **TOOL** capitalizes on the divisiveness and hidden (or obvious) agendas within the team. *STRATEGY¹* draws out the competitive ideas. *STRUCTURE²* enables the team to come back together and develop cohesive, in-depth evaluation and collaboration that promotes both thoughtful dialogue and creative exchanges in order to capture the best ideas.

5

COMPLACENCY / STATUS QUO

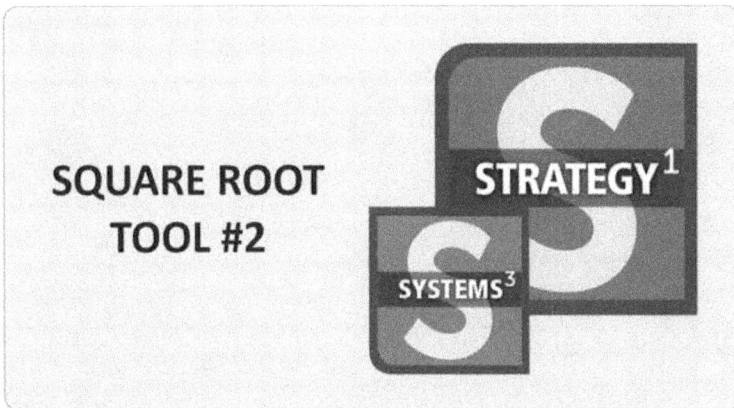

SQUARE ROOT
TOOL #2

STRATEGY[1]

SYSTEMS[3]

"Failure is not fatal, but failure to change might be."

—John Wooden

(Basketball's Coaching Legend)

EXAMPLE: A global, publicly-traded computer company continued operating throughout the 1990's, just as it had in the late 1980's when it was developing its global brand. The CEO and top-leaders were focused on one division of the company to the detriment of the most profitable divisions. Those divisions operated as they always had, while their customers and the competition changed, and their market-share ranking continued to plummet.

KEY ISSUES:

1. Complacent/status quo thinking and behavior.

2. The need to speed up organizational changes to meet market needs and be viable in the long-term.

GOAL:

- *To combat complacency and status quo thinking and actions, and speed up the adoption of the necessary organizational changes.*

STRATEGY[1]: *The core approach the organization will use to achieve its goals.*

Whether complacency is obvious in one member or several members of the team, delaying immediate action will cascade the problem dramatically. My *STRATEGY[1]* was to create urgency and push team members outside of their comfort zone. To achieve this, we set firm meetings, established progress reviews, and implemented deadlines on turnaround timeframes that sustained pressure and propelled momentum. Leaders can drive the key initiatives by shortening timelines and locking-down project deliverable milestones. Even adding public reviews with top-level managers at critical intervals can increase psychological pressure, pushing complacent members to complete their project deliverables, and reinforce further accountability or negative exposure in front of the "top brass."

SYSTEMS[3]: *The coordinated methods that manage the team's energy, creativity, knowledge, experience and commitment to achieve its objectives, and drive overall company success.*

In this complacent organization, bonuses were automatically expected every six months. Bonus achievements were set low and were based only on narrow functional outcomes versus being rewarded for the division's or organization's success.

When tackling a challenge such as this, a bonus structure can be designed that rewards substantial, individual team contributions, and ultimately <u>supports the organization's success.</u>

Bonus Structure

The bonus we designed was structured as follows: 50% of the bonus pool would be available when the team achieved its initiatives. The other 50% of the bonus would be split evenly with each of the team members who *individually* contributed to the success of the team.

As an example, and for easy round number discussions, let's say there are ten people on the team, and the team bonus pool is $100,000.

This means that $50,000 would be available to be divided 10 ways ($5,000 each) when the *team* successfully completes its initiative.

SCENARIO 1: The team did not achieve its objectives. No <u>team bonus</u> was paid; therefore, no <u>individual bonus</u> was available.

SCENARIO 2: The *team* achieved its objectives.

This means the $50,000 bonus for team success was divided 10 ways (five-thousand dollars ($5,000) to each team member.)

The remaining $50,000 was made available and split equally with the individual *team* members who *actively* and *fully* contributed to the <u>success of the team</u>.

SCENARIO 3: The *team* achieved its goals, but only eight of the ten team members delivered successfully. The team received its $50,000 bonus ($5,000 per member) BUT the other $50,000 was split eight ways instead of ten (as there were two members who didn't perform). Those who contributed individually each received an additional $6,250.

The total bonus for each of the eight *fully-performing* team members was: $11,250.00

The two *non-performing* team members received only $5,000.00

By implementing new **SYSTEMS**[3], the leader can raise the bar on when, and under what circumstances, the team can receive a future bonus. As the leader, you can work with your human resources representatives to set the bonus deliverables very high. Team bonus payouts based on active engagement and contribution can be added as incentives for each team member to step-up. Instead of low-level department outcomes, bonuses can be set so they are based on the success of the broad business objectives. The performance standards can include key metrics, accountability and the high expectations the leader establishes upfront. These expectations can be reinforced at regular intervals throughout the team process.

BENEFIT: The ***STRATEGY*[1]*/SYSTEMS*[3] **TOOL** assists leaders who need to compress timelines and speed up the specific output that will positively impact the organization. By designing positive reinforcement through bonus incentives, leaders foster individual accountability that creates urgency and leverages their team's achievements. This **TOOL** drives the message that doing business "the same old way" will not attain success in the new, strategic, results-driven organization.

For a FREE PDF download of the SQUARE ROOT TOOLS^{TM}
Quick Reference Guide
Click Here or Go To: *www.QuantumLevelSuccess.com*

6

'ROUND HERE THINKING

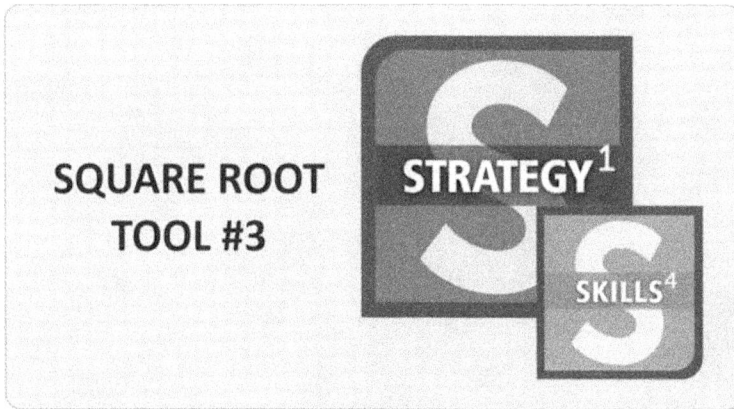

SQUARE ROOT TOOL #3

STRATEGY[1]

SKILLS[4]

"There are two ways of exerting one's strength; one is pushing down, the other is pulling up."

—Booker T. Washington

(American educator, author, orator and political leader)

EXAMPLE: A global company announced a number of initiatives that included new systems, processes and standard operating procedures that could put the organization on a stronger path to sustainable, profitable growth and improved customer satisfaction. The focus was on a number of key initiatives which would immediately promote enterprise-wide organizational involvement and support the future direction of the company. Across the globe, the majority of country leaders supported and pushed the implementation of these initiatives. One country, however, did not and a few country leaders and employees adopted a "this won't work here" attitude.

KEY ISSUES:

1. Select leaders around the globe refused to implement the new key initiatives.

2. The need to strengthen the organization-wide training and adoption of the business improvement measures.

GOALS:

- *To remove the barriers preventing adoption of the key initiatives so that consistent, standard operating procedures could be implemented across the globe.*

- *To strengthen and reinforce positive organizational adoption of the new vision.*

In this challenge, 'Round Here Thinking is defined as the belief (followed by behaviors) that a specific process, solution or plan will not work "here". It won't work "here" because, in this mindset, "here" is unique and different and does not operate like any "there" in the world. Any solution or new process could in no way, not possibly, ever work "here" because "our" customers / procedures / market needs / fill-in-the-blank, etc. are different. 'Round Here Thinking is a show-stopper; a wall to forward progress and must be dealt with.

STRATEGY[1]: *The core approach the organization will use to achieve its goals.*

The **STRATEGY[1]** in this challenge is for the leader to help remove the perceived barrier of "differences" so the company can operate as a broad-based, single entity *everywhere* it serves its customers. As the leader, you can engage the team in an exercise that involves identifying each supposed "difference" and the associated detailed explanation of how it is unique. An effective way to address this challenge head-on is to begin with two white boards or Post-It sheets, one titled, "Regional Differences" and the other, "Global Similarities", (or whichever differences/similarities headings best cater to your needs). One by one, have your team members identify each supposed "difference" and provide the reason(s) for why it is unique. Once the list is exhausted, the leader can challenge the rest of the team members from other regions, countries and functional departments to consider if the supposed "difference" applies anywhere in their operations.

Differences to Similarities

In the majority of the cases, a "difference" *does* apply in another country or region. Therefore, by engaging the team to evaluate the proposed "barrier" together, the assumed "difference" is recognized as being a "similarity", and is, therefore, no longer a barrier.

When the above process is completed, the leader can engage the team in strategically linking each discovered "Similarity" to the company's vision. By focusing the team on how the "Similarities" are connected to the corporate platform, they are better aligned to do their work.

Ultimately, there are far less differences than similarities, so maintaining the focus on similarities and the connection to the new vision, direction and goals of the organization will drive affiliation.

SKILLS[4]: *The excellence of knowledge, unique ability, practice, competence, experience and spirit of cooperation an individual brings to the team.*

Since this company's long-term success requires operating as a global company instead of one that operates as multiple, singular organizations, fresh **SKILLS[4]** are necessary in order to propel this new structure forward. Even the process of operating as cross-functional teams has not been part of the company's day-to-day operating environment. However, operating as fluid cross-functional teams will be imperative going forward and therefore, different social and functional skills will be required.

New Thinking And Focus

Training is powerful in introducing new ways of thinking and operating and helps keep employees energized and fresh. Communications are critical as they underscore the positive effects of operating in the new direction, and in this situation with a consistent focus on its customers' needs. By driving organizational understanding of the key benchmarks, customer satisfaction and loyalty scores, and the products or services that are important to its customers, parochial thinking can be replaced with the real understanding of, and desire for, the organization as a whole to succeed.

BENEFIT: The ***STRATEGY¹/SKILLS⁴* TOOL** removes barriers by focusing the organization on its similarities and promoting enterprise-wide organizational alignment on the new initiatives. Generally, once barriers are removed, mindsets are opened and training can be introduced.

Training presents new ways of thinking and operating, and company-wide communications tie together and reinforce progress. Intermittent training ensures that employees will have the polished skills that will enable them to meet the demands of the changing marketplace. Furthermore, employees become engaged, are flexible and able to maintain a laser-focus on their customers. Training and positive feedback builds morale and motivation. Removed barriers, polished, new-found skills and the associated boost in employee morale ensure short-term wins. Short-term wins diminish the volume of cynics and leverage progress that increases the passionate and enthusiastic delivery on objectives across the organization. "Like eating an elephant, you do it one bite at a time."

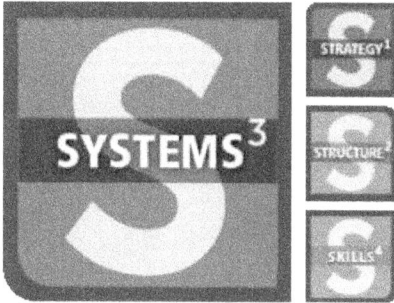

7

POWER COALITIONS

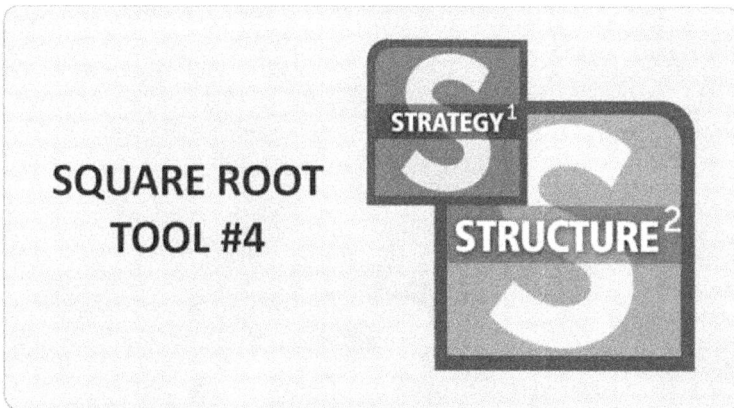

SQUARE ROOT TOOL #4

STRATEGY[1]

STRUCTURE[2]

"Intention is a force in the universe, and everything and everyone is connected to this invisible force."

— Dr. Wayne W. Dryer
(Internationally renowned author and speaker:
The Power of Intention)

E**XAMPLE:** A global medical devices company underwent a major restructure. Historically, this company operated five divisions, each with its own culture and operating procedures. In each sales territory, three or four sales representatives (each from different divisions) sold a device that catered to a specialty, (i.e. cardiology, orthopedics, neurosurgery, etc.) This restructure model was designed to streamline the company's selling processes and create better value to its customers. This new structure required each representative to handle <u>all</u> company products within their territory. Furthermore, this new structure required that the formerly large regions be broken-up and replaced with smaller regions that blended a representative from each division.

Transition

During this *transition* there was tremendous confusion, poor communication and no developed standard operating procedures. The representatives were charged with selling the devices before compensation plans were in place. There were no clear answers and quotas on all products were set extraordinarily high. To make matters more difficult, this change was taking place in an economy where medical reimbursement was down and insurance company authorizations had declined significantly. One of the most debilitating factors was that, due to poor standard operating procedures within the company, a great deal of the individual sales representatives' time was spent dealing with the department that pursued insurance authorizations, which crippled their time on the street and their ability to sell more services. During this time, doctors' offices became frustrated with lag times and confusion over which rep to contact, and threatened to switch to the competition. Customer service was compromised, morale was down, turnover became high, and stress levels were significant. Just as in the emergency room when there are patient warning signs and subtle behavior changes that signal the need for prompt attention, warning signs in organizations and on teams signal the need for intervention.

As humans, when we feel emotional pain we reach out to others for support. The professional friendships that had been formed before the regions were broken-up became even stronger during this chaotic time. Representatives called each other to vent their frustrations and sought guidance from their former teammates, rather than from their newly appointed leaders or even their *new* teammates. Despite the leaders' intentions to build new teams that coalesced and worked together, leaders were stonewalled by the power coalitions that had formed through the formerly established professional friendships. Power coalitions are a small group of members who "circle their wagons", deferring mostly to each other, and withholding acknowledgement or feedback to members outside of their "clique". How can leaders address power coalitions within a team or company?

Magnify Positive Team Behaviors

While it is obvious there are *many* issues that could be addressed, as the team leader you can choose which of the team challenges to face head-on, and choose the associated **TOOL™** that will magnify and reinforce positive team behaviors and outcomes.

KEY ISSUES:

1. A Power Coalition was impeding a cohesive and unified team dynamic.

2. The need to understand the power coalition in order to address some of their underlying needs, while at the same time advancing the teams' success.

GOAL:

- *To neutralize or remove the influence of the power coalition and promote full team engagement.*

STRUCTURE²: *How people in the organization are positioned, coordinated and aligned to utilize their skills and strengths.*

It is important to understand the psychology behind a power coalition. The complexities of human behavior are just that – complex. It is imperative to have the awareness and understanding of psychological and emotional needs when dealing with this challenge. Power struggles are often a manifestation of a person or group that wants to maintain its historic stature, or is an attempt by a person or group to project a perceived "higher authority" within the team or organization. When a power coalition exists on a team, leaders can neutralize its influence quickly by breaking up the alliance.

Neutralize Negative Power

To be most effective, the leader may need to change the team **STRUCTURE²** by removing or replacing some of the coalition members early-on, which can eliminate or diminish its strength. If the leader is required to keep the assigned members on this team, one approach is to pair members from the coalition with other team members. While this approach does not entirely remove the ability for one member of the coalition to defer to another, it does neutralize that person's power by imposing interactions with team members outside of the coalition.

STRATEGY[1]: *The core approach the organization will use to achieve its goals.*

While I am not a psychologist, I have spent much of my time as a leader observing behaviors both inside and outside of the workplace. The **STRATEGY[1]** I have found to be most effective is to single out a person or small group and lavish them with one-on-one meetings and individual attention. These regular meetings - outside of team meetings - are used to galvanize support and embrace this member/these members, which psychologically is important. You have heard the phrase, "If you can't beat them, join them." In this **STRATEGY[1],** the leader engages these members but on the *leader's terms*, and in a way that helps address some of the power coalition team members' underlying needs, which inevitably, advances the teams' success.

BENEFIT: STRUCTURE[2]/STRATEGY[1] promotes full team involvement and aligns the team on the objectives and initiatives before them. **STRUCTURE[2]** neutralizes or removes the power force, and **STRATEGY[1]** fosters engagement and cooperation in a way that benefits the team, as well as those within the power coalition.

STRATEGY[1]   STRUCTURE[2]

SYSTEMS[3]   SKILLS[4]

8

PIRANHA FACTOR

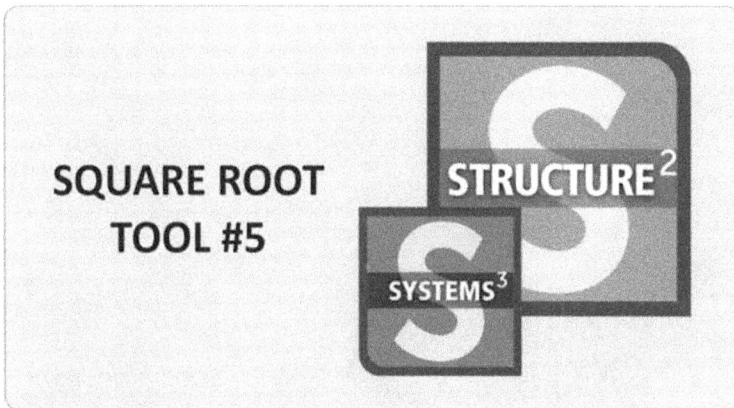

SQUARE ROOT TOOL #5

STRUCTURE^2

SYSTEMS^3

"Peace is not the absence of conflict; it is the ability to handle conflict by peaceful means."

—Ronald Reagan
(The 40th President of the United States, Governor, Actor)

B**ACKGROUND:** There are two kinds of piranhas in this world; the flesh-eating, freshwater fish found in South America, and those on teams who sabotage collaboration, interrupt the free exchange of ideas and destroy team success.

Imagine standing on a bridge overlooking a river in Brazil. While watching below, you drop a chunk of raw meat into the water. Immediately the water begins to churn, followed by ocean-like wakes as tail fins, backs of fish, and whale-force splashes erupt. What most people may not know is, in their fight to get to the meat, the piranhas sometimes eat each other in order to remove the perceived "obstacles" as they fight to reach the prize.

Now, imagine a similar scenario during team meetings. This behavior creates such internal conflict that without being addressed immediately, it leaves the project (and sometimes the team) in shreds. In the majority of cases, this person (the piranha) must be removed from the project, which is certainly the fastest and easiest solution. But what if, as the team leader, you inherited this person? What if you have been instructed to find a way to "keep and work with" this person who, some believe, has the capability to add significant niche value?

Destructive Team Behavior

One of the most difficult and destructive team behaviors to deal with is this type of person, who deliberately uses manipulation, coercion and sabotage for their personal gain. This behavior, when carried into the career environment, I refer to as the "Piranha Factor". When a leader is required to keep a person on a team, despite their personality and ulterior motives, team success can be destroyed unless intervention is taken. No matter how strong your leadership skills, how charismatic your personality, or how fluidly you negotiate, this type of behavior will require much time and attention.

EXAMPLE: A decision-maker was assigned to a cross-global, cross-functional team to address the integration of a new company website. Everything was on the table; new IT architecture, website functionality, and content and translation into seven languages. The CEO mandated that the completed website "go-live" in five months. To achieve an initiative of this magnitude required that decision-makers for each function be present at every bi-weekly meeting.

The piranha-personality in this scenario was actually one of the decision-makers. This person rarely attended meetings, sending in their place a delegate who had no power to make decisions or even speak for this decision-maker. All the delegate could do was to take the information back to this person and "communicate" decisions once they were made. (As you can imagine, no decisions or communications followed.) On the occasion that this decision-maker did attend a meeting, they contributed very little, even when specifically addressed, or was extremely dismissive and caustic in responding to other members' ideas and inputs. Ultimately, this decision-maker pushed for a design and structure of the website that, in the long-term, could not be cost-effective and would sabotage the goal of having a simple streamlined approach.

Emboldened Negative Behaviors

Other team members knew these decisions were counterproductive to the organization's sustained success, but since they directly or indirectly reported to the piranha-personality, they did not challenge this person while in these meetings. This person was further emboldened in her actions because she was involved in an intercompany dating relationship with the president of a region.

KEY ISSUES:

1. A strong personality who exerts his/her status within the company to intimidate members and impede the success of the team.

2. The need to address the strong personality professionally and respectfully, while continuing to inspire the team, enabling them to succeed.

GOALS:

- *To address the challenge of "piranha behavior".*
- *To hold each individual accountable for his or her behavior.*
- *To reward those who promote positive, full-team engagement.*

STRUCTURE²: *How people in the organization are positioned, coordinated and aligned to utilize their skills and strengths.*

The primary approach I took in addressing the piranha personality challenge was through **STRUCTURE²**. In this case, restructure. I moved the offending personality to an *assumed* role outside of their comfort zone. And, I also figuratively "transferred" *each* person (not just the piranha personality) to an *assumed* role far outside of his or her day-to-day functional expertise.

Let's create a team to help illustrate this concept. In addition to me as the leader, the team included Sue, Director of H.R. (the piranha personality); Krishna, IT/Business Development Leader; Sam, HR Manager (who reported to Sue); Miguel, Engineer; and Bob, Finance Manager. For the purpose of operating on this team, and to address piranha challenges, all team members were figuratively assigned new roles. Bob (Finance Manager) assumed the role as Director of I.T.; Miguel (Engineer) assumed the role as Director of H.R.; Sam (HR Manager) was now "working" in the role of Business Development Manager. Krishna (Business Development Manager) was assigned the role of Engineer. And, Sue (Director of H.R. and the piranha-personality) was assigned to the role of Finance Manager. In this illustration, Sam now no longer reported to Sue.

NOTE: *Addressing structure in this way is essential so that no one on the team be placed a subordinate position. This allows the team members the opportunity to share unadulterated, free-exchanges of creative thoughts, ideas and solutions, without having to worry about potential repercussions from his or her "boss" (as the "boss" position has been removed).*

In this new **STRUCTURE**^{2}, each team member was able to bring the strengths, experience and knowledge of their primary role within the company. They assumed the role, perception and rationale of the new function, which broadened their thinking beyond their accustomed boundaries. This structure also served to remove personal loyalties and enabled team members to collaborate without compartmentalized "blinders" or the "intimidation" of a chain-of-command reporting structure.

New Perspective

A by-product of this approach is that in this assumed role, team members can glean a new understanding of the complexity of the issues before them. For example, marketing promotions have associated costs.

High-quality marketing efforts and affordability are not mutually exclusive and must be addressed as part of the solution equation. Placing someone from a marketing department into an assumed finance role provides an opportunity to see first-hand the overall initiative from a different perspective.

(NOTE: *Utilizing* **STRUCTURE**[2] *in this way is highly effective in dealing with passive producers. When passive producers witness members from other functions actively transforming information and delivering vital service ideas, an internal wake-up call sets off an alarm that their "comfortable territory" is threatened. Most will heed the alarm.*)

SYSTEMS[3]: *The coordinated methods that manage the team's energy, creativity, knowledge, experience and commitment to achieve its objectives, and drive overall company success.*

Now that the team is restructured, leaders can design a bonus plan that will reinforce this action. When leaders design a bonus plan for any team, it is important to decide if they will be rewarding collective behavior and winning as a team, or if the success of the team also requires individual contributions and performance. When the team's success also hinges on individual input and behavior, then measuring individual actions must also be factored into the design of the bonus system.

Everyone wants to be valued for his/her skills and contributions, and each member has an idea about how to achieve shared goals. But, if you are treating everyone equally, those who don't perform won't have a large enough incentive, and those who do perform won't be getting enough support. The leader can design the team bonus in a way that amplifies successful team performance, while also holding individual team members' behavior accountable.

BONUS SYSTEM EXPLANATION: The bonus system for our fictional team (above) will be split 50/25/25. Fifty-percent (50%) is available only if the *team* achieves its initiatives. Then 25% is used to award individual performance based on WHAT (the *content* contributed) he/she accomplishes, and the other 25% is based on HOW (the *manner* in which) he/she accomplishes it. In this case, the team's success hinges on individual input and behavior; therefore, measuring individual actions can also be factored into the reward design.

Using round numbers, let's say there are eight people on the team and the team bonus pool is $100,000. In this challenge, the bonus split is 50/25/25; 50% based on team success, 25% based on the individual's WHAT contribution and 25% based on the individual's HOW contribution.

This means $50,000 is available to be divided eight (8) ways ($6,250 each) when the team successfully completes its initiative.

SCENARIO 1: The team *did not* achieve its objectives. No team bonus is paid; therefore, no individual bonus is available.

SCENARIO 2: The *team* achieves its objectives.

This means $50,000 of the bonus for *team* success is divided eight (8) ways. Six-thousand two-hundred-fifty dollars ($6,250) is paid to each member for his/her contributions to the team's success.

Now that the team reached its goal, the remaining $50,000 for individual achievement is available. Twenty-five thousand ($25,000) will be split with each member who actively and fully contributes to the success of the team, and

$25,000 will be split with each member who contributes <u>in a positive and respectful manner</u>.

In this scenario, every individual member fully contributed. All team members stepped up, giving great performances in both the WHAT and HOW categories. Therefore, the total amount that each team member receives in this scenario is $12,500 ($6250 for *team* achievement, plus $3,125 for what they contributed, plus $3,125 for *how* they contributed).

SCENARIO 3: In this scenario, the team achieves its goal. All eight (8) team members receive $6,250 for the *team* achievement bonus.

The remaining $50,000 is split $25,000 for WHAT and $25,000 for HOW. Only seven (7) of the eight (8) team members delivered the WHAT; therefore, each of the seven members received an additional $3,571. Only six (6) of the eight (8) team members delivered in a genuine and respectful manner; therefore, each of the six members received an additional $4,167.

6 of 8 team members received . . . $ 13,988.00

1 of 8 team members received . . . . $ 9,821.00

1 of 8 team members received . . . . $ 6,250.00

Splitting the bonus 50/25/25 adds incentives for each team member to collaborate and genuinely step up to the challenge. Those who do are rewarded for their efforts, teamwork and active contributions.

BENEFIT: The ***STRUCTURE²/SYSTEMS³* TOOL™** leverages ideal team dynamics where deep communication, high collaboration, authentic engagement, and strong execution are fostered. Negative behaviors like intimidation, disrespect, contempt or disregard are not rewarded or supported. This **TOOL™** can also be used when there is a negative, dominating personality or an imposing, overbearing member who uses their title or position to intimidate member contributions, which stifles or destroys team success. By removing the distraction of behaviors or the obstacles of personalities, the team is able to focus on the issues at hand and the leader is able to get the results he/she needs.

> *"Cooperation is the thorough conviction that nobody gets there unless everybody gets there."*
> —Virginia Burden
> (Author of *The Process of Intuition*)

For a FREE PDF download of the SQUARE ROOT TOOLS^{TM}

Quick Reference Guide

Click Here or Go To: *www.QuantumLevelSuccess.com*

9

STRONG SILOS

SQUARE ROOT
TOOL #6

STRUCTURE^2

SKILLS^4

"Team members have to be focused on the collective good of the team. Too often, they focus their attention on their department, their budget, their career aspirations, their egos."

— Patrick Lencioni
(Author of national best-seller
The Five Temptations of a CEO)

When a major change takes place in a company (such as the appointment of a new CEO, a strategic re-structure of an organization, a turnaround or a major acquisition) it is important to understand and build a network of relationships that support the leaders' success. When faced with an organizational transition, or any event that involves major change, you will find three groups: *Supporters, Resisters,* and the *"Mushy-Middle"*.

Supporters tend to automatically approve of the plan and corporate strategy. Perhaps it's because they approve of the new direction, or maybe because they respect the new leader. Maybe they recognize that whatever happened before wasn't working and the new plan makes sense. On the other end of the spectrum are resisters. *Resisters* resist or oppose because that is what they do. *Resisters* often do not like, or want, change. Maybe the change in direction will threaten their role in a company and they antagonize the change efforts. Maybe they fear that a new CEO or a re-structure endangers their power and control, makes their skills obsolete, or their opinions out of synch with the new vision.

The Mushy-Middle

The third category is where you will find the "Mushy-Middle". This includes those who can be persuaded or influenced to embrace the new direction. Often on an issue, 10-percent support change, 10-percent oppose, and 80-percent are somewhere in the middle. The "mushy-middle" is where the majority of efforts should be concentrated.

Significant time and effort certainly need not be exerted on those who automatically oppose because, for the most part, it is a lose-lose effort. Little time need be exerted on those who already support the issues. The best use of communications outreach, resources, and message drive is to focus them on the 80-percent that have the potential to be convinced.

EXAMPLE: A new CEO was appointed to a large global company. This CEO's new vision for the company included the implementation of fresh policies, procedures, and initiatives, which replaced the old ways of doing business. Previously, the company worked as individual silos. The president in charge of business in Spain, who reported to this CEO, had instructed his direct staff to continue operating as they always had, and not implement the CEO's new initiatives. Furthermore, this president manipulated the situation by instructing his staff to act as if they were cooperating. They were to attend the global, cross-functional team conference calls, commit to nothing, and report back what was discussed. Over time, it was made clear through the lack of adoption of the new initiatives that this country's leaders were operating in a "business-as-usual" mode.

(NOTE: *The example below is a situation I witnessed while in a leadership role, and was highly impressed. I saw it as an effective example to utilize in illustrating this **TOOL**™.)*

KEY ISSUES:

1. A strong personality in a leadership position who exerted his status to block the global implementation of the company's new initiatives.

2. The need to drive new, global organizational direction.

3. To provide supervised training that supports the new direction where needed.

GOALS:

- *To add additional reporting layers and accountability.*

- *To provide deeper understanding of, and new capabilities that would support, the implementation of the organization's initiatives for its long-term success.*

STRUCTURE[2]: *How people in the organization are positioned, coordinated and aligned to utilize their skills and strengths.*

In this case, the CEO realized what was happening and knew that the country-based president fell into the resister category, which was detrimental to the long-term success of the company. Therefore, the CEO created a regional director position, to which each country-based president in Europe would report. This modification accomplished two objectives. First, it diminished the prominence and stature of the country-based president's role, signaling that "operating as you know it" was over. Secondly, it raised the country-based presidents' level of accountability and positioned the intermediary regional director closer to the frontline staff and the customer base. With this level of proximity, the regional director could uncover individual, functional, or silo problems that linked to operational concerns, and allowed a direct line of communication between the regional director and the presidents' direct reports. While some country leaders adapted to the new paradigm, for those who could not adapt, a proverbial "window-seat" or "special assignment" was put in place until an exit strategy could be completed. It was important that it be made clear that no one was exempt from working toward the new organizational goals (versus the former "silo protectionism").

Promoting From Within

Once the attrition was completed, the CEO and regional director were free to promote from within, choosing the rising-stars who demonstrated shared values. They also saw this time as an opportunity to recruit and hire the BEST, who embodied the spirit and possessed the skillsets needed to achieve the company's new vision and direction.

SKILLS[4]: *The excellence of knowledge, unique ability, practice, competence, experience and spirit of cooperation an individual brings to the team.*

Since cross-functional team engagement and their associated dynamics had not been part of the historical day-to-day operating culture, the company made strategic efforts to ensure that all of its employees felt they had a stake in the organization's achievement. Training and retraining was imperative and highly emphasized by the company at this time. Leaders continuously praised and relayed how individuals' *SKILLS[4]* contributed to each regions' and/or functions' overall success.

Cross-global Operations

Learning to operate as a cross-global organization, instead of as strong silos, also required that communications throughout the company be restructured. Communications are critical and are often overlooked as a key platform for training. This company became strategic in their communications. The cascade of key information through town hall meetings, sales conferences, management forums and in-country, in-region CEO-led staff meetings, collectively kept people focused on the future and new vision. They also underscored the positive effects of operating with a global focus on customer needs. Regular communications helped everyone in the organization understand that the transformation initiatives were the shortest path to the goal of becoming a more focused, profitable company.

BENEFIT: This **STRUCTURE^2/SKILLS^4 TOOL** assists organizations involved in serious change. By recognizing those people who are flexible, creative and can grasp the new "big picture" with a "can do" attitude, the organization positions itself on the fast-track to success. Positive feedback builds morale and motivation. This **TOOL™** drives organizational understanding, tightens accountability, and focuses the enterprise on the organization's long-term and sustainable achievements.

10

LIP SERVICE - WALK THE TALK

SQUARE ROOT
TOOL #7

STRATEGY[1]

SYSTEMS[3]

"He who would go a hundred miles should consider ninety-nine as halfway."

—Japanese Proverb

EXAMPLE: The marketing managers in Germany created, translated and printed the marketing materials for the sales leaders in their country. Their materials highlighted products and pricing structures different from those materials created and printed by the marketing managers in France, the UK, Italy and the other pan-European countries in which we operated. One of our global initiatives was to standardize the marketing materials to reflect a single-brand, and the new standardized products and pricing structure. Additionally, through our Six-Sigma efforts, another initiative was to cut costs through economies of scale by designing, developing, translating and then printing the marketing materials using a single provider. A marketing manager attended regular team conference calls and face-to-face meetings. During the meetings she said very little, offering neither support nor resistance to the initiatives we were implementing. At the conclusion of each meeting when the recap of the discussion and next steps were reviewed, she signaled agreement and cooperation. Despite affirmative head-nodding, her follow-through did not happen and when pressed, she stated she had no time to complete the new initiatives "on top of her regular duties". In fact, some of the new initiatives replaced former responsibilities that were now obsolete. While mouthing the words "yes", her actions signaled "no."

KEY ISSUES:

1. A team member who did not follow-through on delivery, creating a barrier to the team's success and the organization's goals.

2. The need to help this member improve her performance and therefore, the team's successful outcome.

GOALS:

- To address and reinforce delivery by objectives.
- To highlight short-term wins and the successes the new initiatives would deliver to the company.

SYSTEMS³: *The coordinated methods that manage the team's energy, creativity, knowledge, experience and commitment to achieve its objectives, and drive overall company success.*

In the lip service challenge, it is important to determine if this behavior is individualized. If and when staff members operate in lip service mode, teamwork is destroyed. In my experience, sometimes all it takes is a discussion, bringing this behavior to light for the employee. But if after direct conversations about the ramifications of not performing takes place, and makes no difference, the leader has to make a choice. Probationary action may be taken, or replacement may even have to be considered. When non-cooperation is broader than a single individual and is reinforced by old factions, a bonus is often effective in motivating and reinforcing delivery-on-objectives.

Dotted-Line Reporting Structure

A bonus system can be designed to support broad organizational actions. With this, leaders can increase individual pressure and accountability to deliver. Another **SYSTEMS³** option is to implement dotted-line reporting. Connecting a lip service member to a corporate functional leader establishes and reinforces new accountability. (NOTE: *In a dotted-line reporting relationship, the functional dotted-line leader to whom the employee now reports does not write the performance review. The dotted-line functional leader does, however, have input on how the person is evaluated, which can affect pay raises or replacement decisions.*)

STRATEGY[1]: *The core approach the organization will use to achieve its goals.*

In order for this team and organization to excel there is no room for private agendas. Head nodding and not following through is a private agenda. A ***STRATEGY[1]*** may be to create a series of short-term wins that demonstrate the power and success of the operational initiatives. By designing a system that highlights and encourages short-term wins, the leader positively fosters engagement and cooperation in a way that benefits the team and the organization. Frequently communicating results across the organization, and publically recognizing broad-based actions that are creating success, encourages employees to step up to the plate and follow through on their responsibilities.

BENEFIT: The ***SYSTEMS[3]/STRATEGY[1]* TOOL** helps root out culpability. It removes barriers that cause the inability to follow-through, and applies pressure on delivery-by-objectives. Dotted-line reporting and/or bonuses create a mechanism for tightening accountability, and assist in gaining positive momentum. Short-term wins inspire the implementation of initiatives and leverage progress that increases motivation.

11

PASSIVE-AGGRESSIVE BEHAVIOR

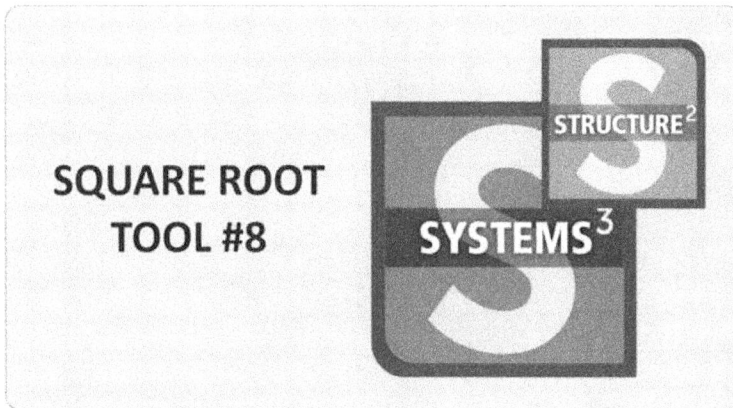

SQUARE ROOT
TOOL #8

STRUCTURE^2

SYSTEMS^3

"Mistrust doubles the cost of doing business. Trust and integrity literally translate into revenue, profits and prosperity."

—Stephen M.R. Covey
(New York Times and #1 Wall Street Journal Bestseller:
The Speed of Trust)

E**XAMPLE:** In a division within a global computer company, a leader with a very strong personality made his ideas known in a "thumbs-up/thumbs-down" final decision, go-forward meeting. When he was out voted 12-1, he made it clear that he was not happy, and took being overruled personally. He then contacted the procurement office and delayed the date of delivery on key computer components.

KEY ISSUES:

1. A team member with a strong personality who used passive aggressive behavior to sabotage the teams' and company's success.

2. To find new ways to move the business forward, despite key issue #1.

GOALS:

- *To address passive-aggressive behavior on this team.*
- *To immediately cease this form of behavior and promote a culture that would support the organization's long-term success.*

SYSTEMS³: *The coordinated methods that manage the team's energy, creativity, knowledge, experience and commitment to achieve its objectives, and drive overall company success.*

It must be understood: Passive-aggressive behavior *cannot* be ignored if success is the goal. Leaders should not allow any person to sabotage an organizational direction. It must be made clear that an individual intent on pursuing his/her own personal agenda at the expense of the team (and ultimately the organization) will not be tolerated. Regardless of how long this person has been part of the company, or how deep the former track-record of achievement has been, it must be made clear that ceasing this destructive behavior immediately is non-negotiable. For the leader, there are no other options.

No "Win-Win" in Sabotage

In the most severe cases, by utilizing the **SYSTEMS³** component, a leader can work with HR to design an exit strategy, severance, or early retirement package for this person. Remove this individual quickly. There is no "win-win" in sabotage. There is a saying in business; "lose fast".

STRUCTURE²: *How people in the organization are positioned, coordinated and aligned to utilize their skills and strengths.*

STRUCTURE² is <u>the</u> component that promotes a culture that will support the organization of the future. Therefore, when a person on a team conducts himself or herself in a passive-aggressive manner, it costs the team. This type of behavior diminishes morale. When people feel threatened by passive-aggressive behavior, they hesitate to share ideas, insights, and information. By removing this behavior, the leader positions the team to coalesce and promotes an environment that leverages the best of the team.

BENEFIT: The *SYSTEMS³/STRUCTURE²* **TOOL** supports leaders in making big changes *fast*. The prompt removal of an individual who blatantly sabotages or poisons the team or company sends a clear message to the team and the organization: *this behavior will not be tolerated.* Leaders can use *SYSTEMS³* to both address negative behavior and instill a success-based company culture. *STRUCTURE²* can be used to support immediate removal and replacement of individuals whose behaviors counteract progress. By quickly making room for rising stars from within the company, or by recruiting leaders from outside the organization, the current leader infuses strength, expertise, and positive momentum, which adds real value and compresses the timeline to achieve success.

12

REGIONAL MISALIGNMENT

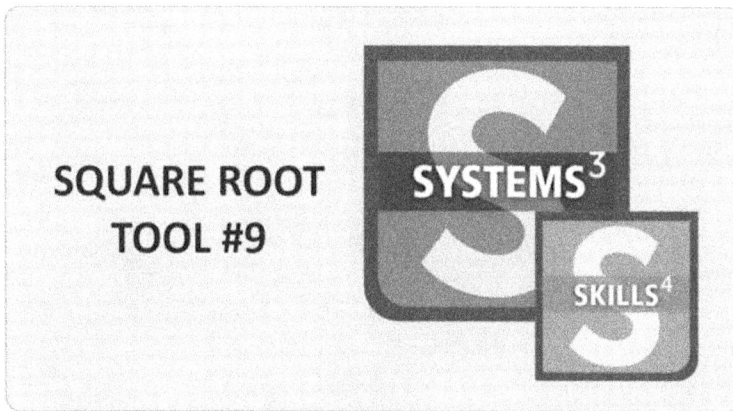

SQUARE ROOT
TOOL #9

SYSTEMS³

SKILLS⁴

"Your present circumstances don't determine where you can go; they merely determine where you start."

—Nido Qubein
(Author/Consultant/Motivational Speaker/Businessman)

EXAMPLE: In one global company, the decision was made to invest heavily in its IT platform in order to seamlessly serve the global company's customers. Part of the investment included standardizing the Information Technology across the globe. In order to achieve this, they had to first understand new business processes that were being rolled-out around the globe, and then program them into the platform. The new business processes, being standardized around the globe, were new to many regional leaders. Unfortunately, global training on these changes was not implemented immediately therefore, some leaders chose *not* to adopt the changes.

Standard operating procedures were developed and implemented across the enterprise. Key metrics and priority benchmarks were established, and state-of-the-art information technology was rolled-out globally, but *only* one region at a time. When the final region was brought on-line, the data clearly revealed that in two critical areas this region lagged far behind the rest of the company in the adoption and implementation of key performance initiatives.

KEY ISSUES:

1. A region's performance on objectives was far below the progress of the rest of the regions (causing a serious misalignment) and negatively impacted the company's results.

2. The managers in this region were not accustomed to the new way of operating, were not properly trained, and therefore, disengaged in implementing the new initiatives.

GOALS:

- *To address misalignment issues within an organization.*
- *To strengthen accountability up and down the organization by driving performance measures that would accelerate positive achievements and leverage success.*
- *To strengthen management abilities and to implement employee training that would ensure success.*

SYSTEMS³: *The coordinated methods that manage the team's energy, creativity, knowledge, experience and commitment to achieve its objectives, and drive overall company success.*

There are several **SYSTEMS³ TOOLS** that can be used to address regional misalignment. Using a bonus system effectively incentivizes people to embrace change, reflect accountability and tie regional performance to the organization's success. Often used in Six-Sigma manufacturing, this approach is effective in cascading metrics down from the corporate level to the front-line employees so that all functional and operational activities are tightly aligned.

Corporate Goals → CEO → Regional / Functional

Directors → Directors → Managers → Front-line

Roll-Up Bonus

In this case, a roll-up bonus payout was designed. A roll-up bonus payout is a framework that begins with corporate goals and is strategically driven down from the top through each level of the organization, all the way to the front-line employees. It is the achievement of the goals at each level that ensures that the organizational strategy, vision, values and direction are unified across all functions and departments. The *achievement* at each level is rewarded through a pre-established financial bonus structure. (Example below)

EXAMPLE: CASCADING ROLL-UP BONUS METRICS	
CORPORATE GOAL	Strengthen market position everywhere we operate
CEO GOAL	No legal judgments against the company in X year
GENERAL COUNSEL GOAL	Improve average control ratings of top-10 risks for company
COMMUNICATIONS GOAL	Develop crisis communications plan for company by X date
MEASUREMENT	Ten chapters of crisis communications plan drafted and approved by legal counsel and sent to CEO by X date

Skip-Level Reporting

Another system that leaders can consider is skip-level reporting, which ensures there will be tight alignment of goals, strategies and actions around the globe or region. In this approach, leaders who are higher in the organization meet with employees who don't directly report to them. These employees are closer to the operations, the front-line, and the customers. This approach avoids isolation from what is really going on inside the company. Supplementing skip-level reporting, offers direct information and feedback (from customers, vendors, partners, suppliers, government officials, etc.). Leaders can determine if, and from where, disconnects within the company may be taking place. One-on-one meetings, staff meetings, functional meetings, and operations and financial reviews, can be stepped up if, and where, necessary. By increasing internal communications through well-developed, two-way processes with employees, leaders are able to share information through a variety of platforms.

SKILLS[4]: *The excellence of knowledge, unique ability, practice, competence, experience and spirit of cooperation an individual brings to the team.*

The globalization of an organization requires **SKILLS[4]** and company culture upgrades. It is important to determine the expertise level of significant managers and directors. If those managers and directors do not possess the tools/understanding required to move forward with the new initiatives, training should be considered. Training strengthens employee skills and abilities, which is vital in order to drive a new culture. It is important to replace those who cannot comply. Training ensures that leaders will be well versed in the changes in products and services, which enables them to communicate this information to all levels of employees. This drives organizational understanding of changes and drives home the benchmarking parameters that are necessary to improve customer service and satisfaction. Leaders who share results and "big wins" across the organization reinforce the focus on key performance metrics. With improved understanding and consistent communications, employees will become more engaged, flexible, and better able to meet the demands of a changing marketplace.

BENEFIT: The ***SYSTEMS³/SKILLS⁴ TOOL*** strengthens accountability up and down the organization and supports the company's focus on performance measures that drive success and accelerate positive momentum. With this approach leaders can drive the passionate and enthusiastic implementation of key initiatives that achieve the integrated, mutually supportive global or regional organization.

13

BLINDNESS TO CUSTOMERS

(INWARDLY FOCUSED ENTERPRISE)

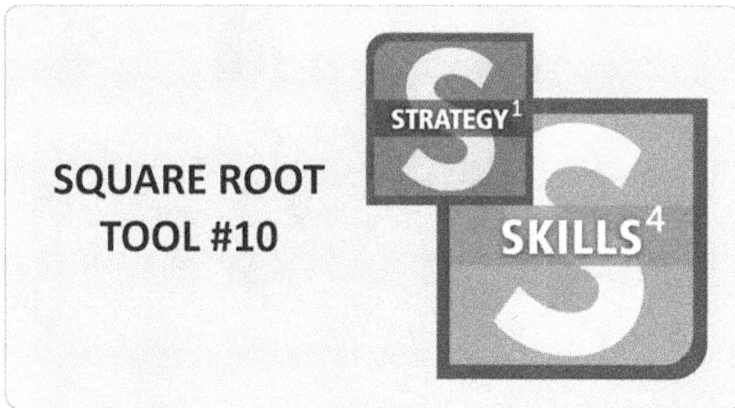

SQUARE ROOT TOOL #10

STRATEGY[1]

SKILLS[4]

"There is only one boss. The customer. And he can fire everybody in the company from the chairman on down, by spending his money somewhere else."

—Sam Walton

(Businessman/Entrepreneur. Founder of Wal-Mart)

T ools and technology have changed how businesses interact. The competitive landscape has also changed dramatically over the past decade. The pace of the market has shortened everything from product life cycles to the migration and adoption of next-generation innovation, particularly in technology. While having the best product or latest technology is still important, it does not, in and of itself, provide a sustainable competitive advantage. Customers want relevant products and value-added services that meet their needs. Therefore, developing improved customer relationships that build long-term trust and compel purchases of your products or services, requires a consistent understanding of each customer's relevant needs, as well as an understanding of what is required to continuously manage that relationship.

EXAMPLE: Following years of market leadership in enterprise hardware systems, a global computer systems company dropped in the marketplace. When the new CEO was appointed to turn this publicly-traded company around, he found an "Ivory-Tower", top-down management style, and an internally-focused organizational culture.

Closed Campus/Closed Thinking

Built on several acres of land outside of the city limits, the headquarters' facilities were isolated and self-contained. Complete with running trails, work-out facilities, state-of-the-art cafeterias, banking facilities and ATM machines, this closed-campus atmosphere contributed to an encapsulated, inwardly-focused culture. The closed-campus environment further created isolation that fed an internal/external misalignment. Because of its location and the way the campus was designed, employees had no need to leave during business hours, which limited networking opportunities. This also dramatically reduced awareness of what was going on outside of the campus, which promoted a "drink-the-Kool-Aid" type of thinking. Adding to this inwardly focused way of doing business was the fact that this company had no systems in place to collect and analyze market or customer data. When external and internal alignment is lost, the organization faces a simple choice; either continue on a slow death path or adapt by making major changes.

KEY ISSUES:

1. A former industry leader became inwardly focused.

2. Top managers had no competence in collecting or analyzing important market shifts, or the ability to use quantifiable data to back-up their business assumptions.

3. Find a new way for employees to engage in business processes going forward.

GOALS:

- *To train necessary personnel on data collection and analysis and, as a company, get a grasp on the ever-changing customer needs and market realities.*
- *To remove the company thinking from within its isolated "bubble", returning it to a market leadership position.*

SKILLS⁴: *The excellence of knowledge, unique ability, practice, compe-*
tence, experience and spirit of cooperation an individual brings to the
team.

This challenge could not be fixed solely from within the organization because this company first had to understand that the marketplace, *not* the technology they designed, defines market opportunities. The marketplace provides insight on variations and trends, signaling changes in customer behavior, competition, and potential future changes in direction.

Everything Begins With The Customer

Many companies spend more time and effort looking at competitors, but the reality is, it starts with the customer. This company needed to learn to ask themselves and their customers, "How can we do better?"; "Where may we have misstepped?"; and, "What will it take to meet and exceed your needs?"

In order to understand where this company was positioned in the marketplace, and to gain a deeper view of the external competitive landscape, the leaders had to engage high-level outside consultants who possessed the *SKILLS⁴* to deliver a complete analysis. The premium was on the rapid and full diagnosis of the business situation, including customer attitudes and opinions, and market and technology changes. This analysis and data broadened the company's understanding of its customers' needs, such as how their customers defined success and envisioned their future growth.

For this company to rise again, the sales team needed to learn new *SKILLS⁴* that would enable them to get closer to their customers, and establish a "valued-partner" status, versus a simple vendor relationship, becoming more involved in their customers' advanced development cycle. Aligning themselves with their customers in this way would allow the company to develop products that mattered most for their customers.

Cultural Shift

To achieve this company's growth potential required putting its customers front-and-center, by meeting or exceeding their expectations in quality, delivery and services. To do this further required a cultural shift from an internally-driven, isolated silo, to a customer-centric, externally driven organization that raised the standards on everything it did. The new focus on data gathering and analysis shed a light on the areas that needed training. This training helped the employees understand benchmarking against industry standards and customer loyalty, competition threats, and marketplace fluctuations. The development and daily tracking of key performance metrics and *rigorous* customer satisfaction tracking was imperative.

Asking questions such as the ones below gave insight into these topics:

- Do we deliver on time?
- Are we low cost?
- Do you (customer) see the value-add?
- Are we considered in your development cycle?
- Are you likely to recommend our services to others?
- How do our pricing levels measure up to the competition?
- How does our service measure up to the competition?

Customer Needs

Tracking and communicating customer needs, customer processes and customer satisfaction and loyalty measures became a consistent practice. Increasing the employees' understanding of customer needs on multiple levels was critical in order to know how to solve its customers' problems, exceed its expectations, and invent solutions that would be critical in driving the company's growth.

Everyone needed to have a stake in the game. Communications included reinforcing how each department supported the company's overall success. This was the beginning of changing the company culture from one that was inwardly-focused to one that was passionate and customer-focused. In actions and in words, the company instilled a new mantra; "when our customers are happy, we WIN."

STRATEGY[1]: *The core approach the organization will use to achieve its goals.*

Once the company had a firm grasp of the analytical data, it was positioned to develop distinct, sustainable strategies. The **STRATEGY[1]** and long-term success of the organization included gathering and utilizing on-going data to maintain an intensive focus on its customers. Leaders utilized this necessary data to develop new policies and operating practices that enhanced its competitiveness, simultaneously changing the company culture from one that was inwardly-focused, to one that was customer-focused. Engineering these improvement measures was as high a priority as any other action.

Promote Rising Stars

Another strategy was to identify and promote rising-stars who would help grow a new line of business. These employees were rewarded for their prompt and passionate performance, and their delivery on objectives was acknowledged company-wide when they embraced the new mantra.

BENEFIT: The **SKILLS[4] / STRATEGY[1] TOOL** is valuable when changing an inwardly-focused, top-down culture to one that is laser-focused on its customers. **SKILLS[4]** training and the emphasis on monitoring the changing marketplace data creates a platform so that leaders can keep their eyes on the vital signs of the organization, and intervene with corrective action if there is a slippage in metrics. **STRATEGY**[1] development concentrates on the actions that will address customer needs and will create a continuous feedback-loop. With this feedback-loop, employees become engaged and better able to meet the demands of a changing marketplace. With visibility into issues, metrics, and behaviors, the accountability bar is raised for management leadership and staff performance on all levels.

14

ENGRAINED "OLD CULTURE"

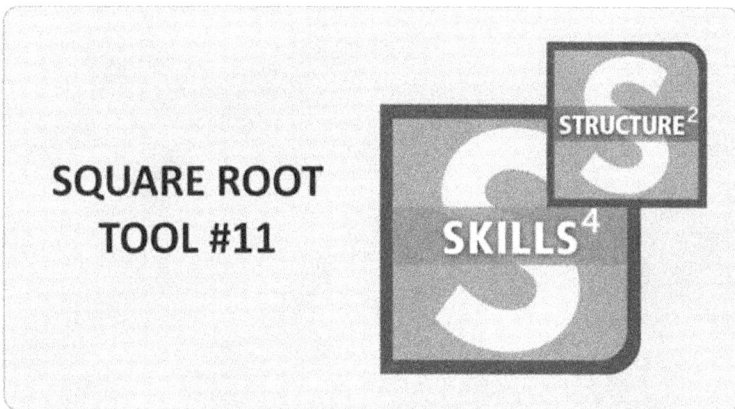

**SQUARE ROOT
TOOL #11**

STRUCTURE^2

SKILLS^4

*"Achieving your vision doesn't mean you've reached
the end of the line. It simply means that you've come
to a new starting place."*

— Nido Qubein
(Author/Consultant/Motivational Speaker/Businessman)

ompany culture reflects the morale of its people, and the decisions, communications, mistakes and victories a company experiences over a long period of time. Implementing a major corporate culture change is one of the hardest challenges. Often, senior managers have been with the company for years and have been promoted to their position from a former one within the company. These managers practice strongly entrenched, cultural patterns. This can present a challenge when it comes time to move forward in a new direction. People who have been with a company for multiple years are often resistant to change and their behavior may reflect and nurture the same culture from which they grew.

EXAMPLE: A culture shift was necessary for a company transitioning from an "old economy" telecommunications monopoly to a company that would be able to compete in a highly-competitive marketplace. Investor expectations and the changing markets drove much of this transformation. Combined with this were other companies throughout the telecommunications industry who all wanted to grab a piece of the (at that time) $100-billion-a-year business.

For this company to develop and establish itself for the long-term, it needed to offer new services in a competitive market that was rapidly introducing new products.

The company I was working with was able to get into Argentina's cellular business before the government began charging for cellular licenses. It was then invited into Israel, where cellular demand was so high, and the lines so long, that one prospective customer threatened to blow himself up with a hand grenade if he had to wait any longer. (NOTE: *He was promptly moved up to the head of the line and no one was injured.*)

KEY ISSUES:

1. A company needed to change from a being a monopoly to having to contend in a highly competitive market.

2. The highly competitive marketplace had multiple, well-financed competitors.

3. It was necessary for the company to expand outside of its traditional borders in order to grow.

GOALS:

- *To train and instill new management styles that could meet the new direction of the company.*
- *To recruit leaders who could grow the business in new markets.*

SKILLS[4]: *The excellence of knowledge, unique ability, practice, competence, experience and spirit of cooperation an individual brings to the team.*

Dealing with an engrained old culture challenge is a little tougher because the senior managers in this scenario were smart, dedicated, top-level leaders who, through years of hard work, contributed to the company's success. Yet, in order for the company to be successful in the future, the engrained and former management styles needed to be replaced in order to support the new direction of the company.

Competitive Environment

This company's long-term success required operating in a competitive environment where flexible and customer-focused responsiveness was needed to replace a slow and staid monopolistic manner. To achieve this, fresh **SKILLS**[4], approaches and thinking were required. As the business context changed, employees were asked to adapt how they thought, behaved and acted. At this company, every meeting (and I mean <u>every</u> meeting) began with the picture of a house and the question, "How can we deliver more products and services to gain a bigger portion of each home?"

New Ways of Thinking

We know that training and communications introduce new ways of thinking and operating and keeps employees energized and fresh. In this company's case, managing for a competitive environment required new skillsets. When a company aligns its communications with its business priorities and provides its people with the open communications needed in order to build their confidence, it fosters their ability to help transform the company. Communications are critical as they underscore the positive effects of operating in a new direction, the focus on customer needs, and the course of the company in the competitive market.

STRUCTURE[2]: *How people in the organization are positioned, coordinated and aligned to utilize their skills and strengths.*

When a company grows outside of its comfortable boundaries (whether it grows from Atlanta to Miami, or from Atlanta to Argentina), people from the new locations can and should be recruited into leadership roles within the company. Those leaders are best able to bring local market information, language, and culture to the company, while simultaneously bringing the company's products, services, and culture to the local markets. Additionally, those leaders recruited new hires who would support the new direction of the company, and bring in the enthusiasm, creativity and problem-solving skills necessary to address that local market (such as having the cultural knowledge to know how to negotiate with a person holding a hand grenade.)

New Direction

As discussed in previous challenges, it may be necessary to replace those who cannot adapt to a new direction. In this case, long-term managers were deeply entrenched in the former culture and continued a rigid hold on old ways. Leaders developed the solutions necessary to replace them, and made room for new, flexible, high-potential leaders. "Reward the best, remove the rest."

BENEFIT: The **SKILLS^4/STRUCTURE^2 TOOL** is useful when a company comes to a point that it must retrain and restructure its personnel in response to a changing marketplace. **SKILLS^4** training brings its employees current with a rapidly emerging, highly-competitive market. **STRUCTURE^2** provides the opportunity to make changes rapidly and bring in leaders with fresh insights, driving the needed dynamic changes for the company to succeed in its business ventures.

STRATEGY[1] STRUCTURE[2]

SYSTEMS[3] SKILLS[4]

15

"LAGGING BEHIND"

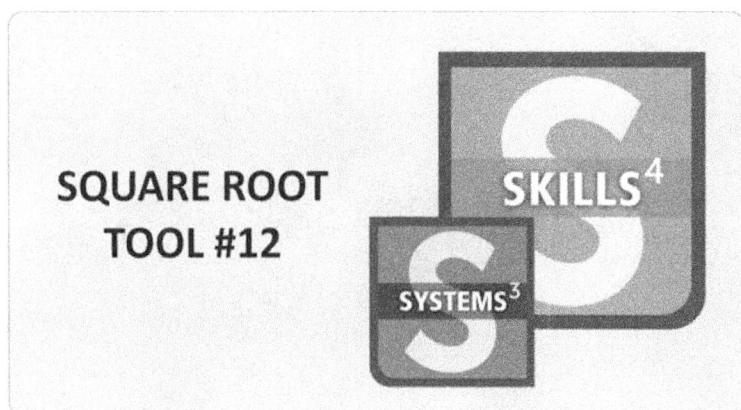

SQUARE ROOT
TOOL #12

SKILLS⁴

SYSTEMS³

"When everyone on the team is accountable, the team's effectiveness rises above the sum of its parts. Each team member doesn't just do what is asked, but what is needed."

–John J. Murphy
(Author: *Pulling Together*)

EXAMPLE: When one part of the organization moves forward, and another part of it lags behind, the organization's progress and momentum are thwarted. This challenge occurs when the communications cascade is disrupted or stopped. It can also occur when a division leader is skeptical about the real possibilities of achieving the organization's new strategies, or is not truly committed to sustaining the energy and actions necessary for the organization's continued success.

KEY ISSUE:

1. The organization's collective success is interrupted.

GOALS:

- *To re-engage the division that is not keeping pace.*
- *To identify and address the reasons the division's progress is disrupted.*

SKILLS[4]: *The excellence of knowledge, unique ability, practice, competence, experience and spirit of cooperation an individual brings to the team.*

In this situation, the first step is to determine what specifically happened to cause the division to lag behind the rest of the organization. The ability to engage in honest communications is a tough skill. However, honest communication is the glue that holds together strong, successful relationships. In this case, the honest communications took place between management and the employees of that division. By discussing and evaluating what caused the momentum to be disrupted, management and employees developed together the necessary solutions. Additionally, once the solutions were implemented, management remained engaged to proactively (instead of reactively) prevent this from reoccurring in any other division.

Strengthening Management Skills

Solving problems and removing barriers does not always come naturally to leaders. In a challenge where part of the company is not keeping pace with a part of the direction, it is important to determine if it is the **SKILLS**[4] level of key leaders that is preventing progress. One way of strengthening management skills where necessary could include providing short-term support (i.e. a mentor). If however, it is found that the cause of the disruption stems back to a division leader's inability to support the direction of the company, it may require a lateral move and replacement with a high-potential, internal performer.

SYSTEMS[3]: *The coordinated methods that manage the team's energy, creativity, knowledge, experience and commitment to achieve its objectives, and drive overall company success.*

Aligning **SYSTEMS**[3] to the company's vision is vital. In this instance, the leader, using the bonus/metrics **SYSTEMS**[3], can create effective incentives and set clear criteria. Face-to-face meetings and frequent divisional operations reviews help monitor progress as the division regains its momentum and becomes aligned with the rest of the organization.

Increasing Communications

Often, organizations make the mistake of slowing down or ceasing communications about the new focus and company direction before the new changes in operating procedures or new culture are *fully* anchored. It may be important to increase internal communications across the company to ensure that all levels of the organization have the information they need to maintain momentum.

BENEFIT: The *SKILLS^4/SYSTEMS^3* **TOOL** can be used to address the disruption of initiatives, or to fix internal misalignment. When an organization can honestly assess where skills, strengths, and weaknesses lie, it can also clearly show where it will be beneficial to implement or tweak *SYSTEMS^3* that may or may not already be in place. By doing so, the organization can *proactively* prevent a disruption in the implementation of its objectives.

For a FREE PDF download of the SQUARE ROOT TOOLS^{TM}
Quick Reference Guide
Click Here or Go To: *www.QuantumLevelSuccess.com*

16

CONCLUSION

Let's face it, challenges arise, unforeseen events transpire and Murphy's Law can tend to rule in spite of the most thought-out plans and objectives. When challenges do arise, it is important to handle them calmly and with authority. By clearly defining the key issues in order of importance you are able to determine which of the **SQUARE ROOT TOOLS™** will make the greatest impact and accelerate your teams' progress. These **TOOLS™** are designed to help you encourage and support your team as together you work through forward-progress and the natural set-backs, until the right creative solutions are discovered.

THE SQUARE ROOT MODEL™ was developed to help you deal with whatever team challenge you may face. Effective leaders analyze each situation and determine which of the **SQUARE ROOT TOOLS™** is best able to leverage the success of the team. Distractions are powerful destroyers of team success and therefore, it is necessary to evaluate and understand which **TOOLS™,** when applied, will effectively manage and provide the greatest possible best outcomes for your team.

Highly-Effective Successful Teams Needed

In the previous pages, we reviewed the challenges of companies who had critical priorities and others whose long-term sustainability was very much in question. We also explored companies that were abundant in resources and others that were lacking in profitability and talent-pool. What they all had in common was the need for highly-effective, successful, highly-performing Power Teams.

Whether your company is global, publicly-held, regionally-based, pressed with competitive environments or has a high barrier to entry, reaching a level of team excellence involves the leaders' ability to cultivate a culture that is conducive to true team functioning. As John Murphy states in his book _Pulling Together_, "Along with clarity in both goals and roles, effective team members understand their responsibility to manage their behavior in line with team rules. This means putting the team first, sharing information and getting involved. When everyone on the team is accountable, the team's effectiveness rises above the sum of its parts. Each team member doesn't just do what is asked, but what is needed."

Through **THE SQUARE ROOT TOOLS™**, leaders are able to build Power Teams where high collaboration, authentic engagement, strong execution and accountability are adopted. High-performance teams increase value to the organization, accelerate growth, enhance innovation, and improve customer relationships and stronger partnering. The quality of leveraged performance drives TEAM achievements that accelerate your organization's long-term successful future.

Team Personalities

Successful teams have similar personalities; just as those that are deadly, non-productive or an outright waste of time have distinct features. We know that the challenges discussed throughout this book are not the only ones we as leaders may come across in an organization.

When utilizing **THE SQUARE ROOT MODEL**™ and its **TOOLS**™, leaders are empowered. **THE SQUARE ROOT TOOLS**™ help you, the leader, drive momentum and deepen each employee's full and creative participation to find solutions that support your team's contributions to the success of the organization. By keeping your finger on the pulse of team changes and implementing **THE SQUARE ROOT TOOLS**™ and its processes, you are able to leverage your teams for success.

Compress Timelines

When implemented, **THE SQUARE ROOT TOOLS**™ help remove divisiveness and hidden agendas, creating an atmosphere of collaboration that promotes creative exchanges and dialogue that foster full team engagement. Furthermore, these **TOOLS**™ can assist leaders who need to compress timelines and speed up output, driving the message that doing business "the same old way" will not achieve success, thus signaling to the enterprise that it is a "new day" and there is a "new way" to operate. Those with ambitious, supportive, growing and vibrant mindsets will be revealed and may even be seen as a candidate for a leadership position in the future.

THE SQUARE ROOT MODEL™, positions leaders so they are able to reinforce actions on objectives, foster transparent relationships, promote full-team involvement and leverage ideal team dynamics. This allows deep communication, high collaboration, authentic engagement and strong execution to be adopted within the team. Negative behaviors become neutralized or can be replaced with behaviors that promote accountability up and down the organization, systematically accelerating organizational understanding and focus on the vision, direction and culture.

Leading a team is both a privilege and a gift. As leaders, we are in a position to foster and grow people to their fullest potential. With compassion and patience (both needed at times) we can discover "why" a person or group is behaving the way they are and then consider how to help each move beyond his or her self to contribute in successful ways. It is in the process of leading, encouraging others and helping them get what they want, while keeping the focus on a vision bigger than each person, that we recognize the value of relationships and their role in our collective achievement. When people come together and act as a team, we collectively have the ability to make a difference.

The gift also comes in the relationships built. Success is a tie that binds. There are many former colleagues who have become very close friends and we stay in touch regularly, though we haven't worked together in a decade or more. I welcome the opportunity to work with them again!

Finally, I love to hear leadership stories, both successes and speed bumps. These challenges, when shared, help us grow. If you care to share your stories, or if you would like to contact me about a particular challenge, please reach me at: deb@quantumlevelsuccess.com.

Live Motivated! Live highly-effective!
Live Your POWER!

ACKNOWLEDGEMENTS

I would like to acknowledge Sarah Spicer, my daughter and personal editor. She has dedicated hours of her time and invested personally and professionally to let me know when my message had big holes, when my intent was not clear, and when she "loved" portions of the manuscript. As a writer and producer in her own right, she is my formidable confidant and can tell me like it is, unlike any other. I am experiencing first-hand the incredible return-on-investment for all of those college funds! Seriously, I am tremendously proud of her as such a bright, beautiful, smart, passionate, driven, determined, caring, compassionate, and full-of-life woman.

I would also like to acknowledge my former incredible teams! We have grown stronger together, learned together, and achieved together. For those who remain close friends, it is because you invested yourself fully, trusting and contributing, that we succeeded. For those who embodied the spirit and behaviors we addressed throughout the book, thank you! It is because of those nuances that we found new ways to succeed.

And, to my loving husband, Mike, who continued to inspire me, my sister, Mary, and dear friends (Brooke, Sara, Julie and Sanjana), thank you for your positive encouragement and outright cheerleading!

Healthcare Deep Dives:

Driving Success through Improved
Patient Delivery and Solid Satisfaction Metrics

Patient satisfaction is receiving greater attention as a result of the rise in pay-for-performance (P4P) and the public release of data from the Hospital Consumer Assessment of Healthcare Providers and Systems (HCAHPS) survey. As well, patients are able to compare hospitals on both patient satisfaction and health outcome measures at HospitalCompare.gov or evaluate hospital performance through Consumer Reports Health Ratings Center.

If you need to:

- Understand factors inhibiting excellent customer service
- Implement accountability and coaching for managers
- Take a fresh look at problem departments
- Explore engagement, process or professional-style issues

For Coaching, Training,
Research or Consulting
Call Today: 321.947.4300

Customer Service Intensity (CSI):

Delivering Higher Levels of Service

Customer loyalty is a major contributor to sustainable profitable growth. Customers today will not be loyal to any business, if the business does not meet their service needs.

A multinational survey of 8,800 companies in 16 countries attributes losses to flawed customer service:

$338.5 billion in aggregated lost business
Each lost relationship costs $243 (average value)
Transactions taken to a competitor — 63 percent
Loses abandoned entirely — 37 percent
We can help

For Customized Customer Service Training, Coaching, Research or Consulting
Call Today: 321.947.4300

Crisis Communications:

Preserving Your Right and Ability to do Business Unfettered

In most crises, the first few hours are critical!

In managing a crisis the overriding concerns are:

1. The public interest
2. The health and safety of the corporation's employees and their families.

Everyone involved should be thoroughly familiar with the corporate-wide sanctioned strategic crisis plan so that it can be put into effect without delay. In addition, most companies are concerned with:

– Protecting its reputation for integrity and corporate responsibility
– Preventing deterioration of the company's financial position in both the short- and long-term
– Minimizing the chances of costly or embarrassing litigation
– Maintaining the company's share of the market
– Preserving the right and ability to do business unfettered

Don't have a strategic crisis plan? We can help.

We will help you:

- Ensure the proper authorities are provided with information needed to protect public and employee safety
- Ensure that accurate information is released to the news media as soon as it becomes available
- Counteract the effects of rumors and inaccurate information
- Ensure that the company speaks with a single voice

Call Today: 321.947.4300

www.ingramcontent.com/pod-product-compliance
Lightning Source LLC
Chambersburg PA
CBHW062006200326
41519CB00017B/4689